what will they call me when I'm gone

a trans poetry
memoir
by Lauren Scott

Wider Perspectives Publishing   ∞ 2025 ∞   Hampton Roads, Va.

©2025, Lauren Scott including writing as Scott Munn
1st run complete in October 2025
Wider Perspectives Publishing, Hampton Roads, Va.
ISBN   978-1-964531-05-2

Dedicated to my friend, Lubna.
You have played a vital role
in shaping me into the woman I am today.
Thank you for everything you have done.

contents

IV   Changing

V   Rising

Lately I've been thinking about when I die

Two minutes ago
  I watched my dog die.

My father
  put the bag
over its head
  with the tube
to the gas
  fed into it.

Through my tears
  my mother tells me
they had to do it.
  He was old and sick,
she says.

She doesn't say it
  out of comfort,
but like someone
  ending an argument
frustrated and exhausted.

the thing is
  I don't remember
my dog dying

  not really

I can't tell you
        what it looked like
when he struggled and kicked
        in those last moments of his life.

I don't remember
        the look
of the bag
        or the shape
of the gas canister.

As if those moments
        are memories
of someone else's life.
a scene pieced together
        in my mind's eye
as they recount the story
        to me.

I can only tell you
        how I felt
and in the end
        that might be all memories are.

what will they call me when I'm gone

We think of life
       as moments
that shape
       our emotions,
but those moments are fleeting
while
       the feeling
lingers

and so
       our lives become
not emotions
       shaped by
moments
       but
moments
       shaped by
those emotions.

Three minutes ago
       I watched my dog die
and in those minutes
       I would like to think
something changed.

That there is some
       distinct, definitive, difference
between that loving creature I knew
       and that lifeless body
that now lies
       limply in our garage.

I like to think
        that there is some essence
some lifeforce
        we carry,
be that
        a soul
or
        something else.

That my life
        is more than
the blood
        and oxygen
coursing through
        my body.

That I am more
        than the parts
that compose me.

I like to think
        however much I doubt it
that I am more
        than this body.

Something intangible
        but undeniably real.

Lately, I've been thinking about
        when I die,
what words they will use
        to describe me.

what will they call me when I'm gone

What name
        will they print

on the tombstone

        in the obituary?

Will they call me
        a brother,
a son?

Will they call me
        by a name
I no longer
        connect to?

 Five minutes ago
        I watched my dog die
and in those three hundred seconds
        something changed,
but I'm not sure I can tell you
        what that was.

what will they call me when I'm gone

I
Freezing

Beauty (from the back of the closet)

She laughs.

She laughs
at the idea
of me
calling myself
Beautiful.

At the idea
of a man
being
Beautiful.

because, clearly,
that's what I am.

A Man.

it would be foolish
to argue otherwise

it's obvious,
from the shape
of my face
and the hair
that hides it.

what will they call me when I'm gone

and maybe
she laughs
because she has
something
I never will

an unquestioned
essence of femininity,
a captivating grace
and elegance
to her shape
and flow

and when I
hear her
I want to
speak out
in indignation.

but a part of me
fears,
knows,
she's right.

I try to push
the thought
to the back
of my mind

far back
and bury it
like a dress
hidden behind
a long, homogenous line
of men's shirts.

pushed deep
back
into the closet,
into my mind

along with
images
of lipstick
pressed and spread
against
my lips.

the look and feel
of my legs
freshly shaven.

because I know
if these ever emerged
from the piles and piles
they're buried underneath,
I might have to bear
that laughter
again.

what will they call me when I'm gone

I want to snatch
that word,

Beautiful

out from between
her smooth, slender fingers,
from her supple, red lips.

to take it
away from her

just briefly,
just to borrow it.

to feel
for a moment
what she feels
everyday
without having
to second-guess
herself.

Maybe then
in that brief moment
I can know
what it means
to be

Beautiful.

In The Present

Stepping into
the room
I know I do not belong
here

I feel their gaze on me
both fearing and knowing
exactly
how they see me

I think back
to this same room
this same occasion
only two years ago

You're a man
at a baby shower.
You already look
ridiculous.

she shouts over to me

Yesterday
I was wrapping the paper
around the box
to cover it completely
to leave no marks
no exposure
to have no excess
no waste

what will they call me when I'm gone

But the corners
don't   touch
the way they need to

something about the dimensions
that I can't get quite right

I think back
to an old Christmas party

A coworker
holds my gift in her hands
and remarks

*This must
have been wrapped
by a woman*

In that moment
I feel a strange mix
of pride and confusion

I need to recreate that scene

But the corners
don't   touch
the way they need to.

Sitting there in that room
one woman
tells me
how adorable I look

another one asks
if I packed the gift basket myself.

A few hours earlier
a student
did a presentation
on Judith Butler and gender.

They thank me
for teaching them
something new.

A few months earlier
I break down
in tears,
feeling unable
to escape
these constraints.

In a couple hours
everything
will be torn
open
and its contents
slowly unpacked.

But I cannot escape
to the future
just yet.

I am still trapped
in the present.

what will they call me when I'm gone

Gay is a dirty word

I thank her for calling me Ms.

I try to keep my eyes dry,
but I know she can hear it
in my voice.

The way it shakes
and quivers.

And in that moment
I hate myself.

*No one should feel good
about accepting me.*

It's a line I have said
over and over,
as if I repeat it
I will eventually
internalize it
and embody it.

I'm told I shouldn't
decorate my classroom
for Pride Month.

They suggest
rainbows
instead.

I watch a teacher
through the screen
of my phone.

She's not allowed
to talk
about her queerness
    in her classroom.

Instead she covers it up
in rainbows.

She talks with a glee
in her voice,
as if she has
gotten one over
on the system.

I want to tell her
through the screen
of my phone
that she lost.

That we compromise
what we consider
a victory
to and for
ourselves.

what will they call me when I'm gone

That it is
pathetic
how much
we restrain,
we restrict,
our own existence
as if by uttering it
too loudly
we threaten to fracture
the thin glass psyches
that have been carefully
crafted and curated
by those who
constrain us.

I show them my
reworked door decorations
for Pride Month.

The ones that don't
have words
that aren't meant to be seen
by children.

Words like gay.
Words like homosexual.

I show them
the piece
with the words

Life
Gets
Better
Together

sprawled in big letters.

They say it's great.
They say they didn't even notice
the acronym
till I pointed it out.

A student tells me
that I shouldn't say
gay.

That it's a bad word.
That it's not appropriate
for school.

what will they call me when I'm gone

I sit there,
a young, quiet child
in the classroom

as one of my classmates
derisively calls something
gay.

The woman behind the desk,
her face framed
by her short brown hair
and her thick rimmed glasses
says that the word
gay
means happy.

Taking her index fingers
she curls her mouth
into an upward crescent.

Even then,
in my cold desk,
blissfully unaware
of my own complexities
and complications
that linger and rest
inside me,

I think of her
as a coward.

Don't ask.
Don't tell.

We want to act
like these words
died years ago.

That they don't
still silently
wrap around
our tongues
and ears.

Kids are too young
to learn about gender,
to understand it,
they tell us

as teachers have
boys
     and girls
line up
in their own
segregated sections.

They don't finish
the thought
or finish
the phrase
because they don't know how,
because they've never been asked to.

what will they call me when I'm gone

I wonder
in those moments

as a student calls me
mister

as another teacher calls me
sir

if there's not some
young, quiet child
that sits there
in my classroom

and thinks of me
as a coward.

what will they call me when I'm gone

II
Flowing

10/31

It's Halloween night. I walk down the street with a short lived set of friends, as we travel from door to door. Occasionally as we pass by, I hear someone say, *Aren't they a little too old to be trick or treating?* I can't say they're entirely wrong. Maybe we haven't gotten the transition down quite right, and maybe I never will.

Halloween offers none of the comfort of consistency you get from Christmas and Thanksgiving. At some point you age out of trick or treating, and you're meant to go to parties. Maybe later on you'll be lucky or well off enough to give kids candy from the other side of the door, or dress up your own children as they go out into the night.

It's a holiday meant to usher in the Fall, a season of transition, where the leaves fade to orange and red as they fall to the ground. I envy the ease at which nature can so readily transform itself.

It's Halloween night and I'm spending it with someone I've known for less than a month and within another month or two will never talk to me again. As we sit on the couch watching the tv, I can't help but think about my dog at home, spending her last moments lying in the driveway with a worn out towel underneath her. By tomorrow morning, she'll be dead.

what will they call me when I'm gone

It's Halloween night and I'm at yet another college party surrounded by people I don't know with the occasional person I barely know mixed in there as well. A guy tells me I'm cute and in a drunkenly flirtatious motion pulls me in as he pushes his lips against mine. In my shock and confusion, I stand there as the people around us pull him off.

He apologizes to me the next morning. I tell him it's fine. I can't say I minded it too much, but I don't have the courage to admit it to anyone.

It's Halloween night. I lay in a hospital bed trying to not focus too much on the guards that have me on suicide watch. One of them tells me I look like someone. When I say Macaulay Culkin, they smile and nod.

I pass the time watching the tv. AMC is playing The Wolf Man. Lon Chaney stumbles through the black and white woods as the silhouettes of trees loom in the background and fog covers the forest floor. I think about how much can change in a single night.

Halloween is that night where we plunge our knives into pumpkins to cut them open and remove everything that has collected inside, to be thrown away, out of the way, to carve a way to a new identity and in that, a source of light. I envy the ease at which it can so readily transform.

It's Halloween night.

When you get there

He's 11 years old, maybe 12, the details are fuzzy. Sitting there on the bus, he leans his head against the glass window. Past that window, dozens of little bodies are flocking from the school. They stop to exchange secret handshakes, final words, or possible plans for later that week. Girls exchange smiles and hugs.

He wonders to himself what it would be like to be among those girls, to share those smiles with them. To be able to say that he was one of them.

Time works in strange ways. When we piece together narratives of our lives, it's always after the fact. Seemingly unrelated events tied together in order to form some semblance of a narrative.

People want something straight forward, something with a clear starting point and destination. But lives don't work that way. Our stories aren't chronological, they're winding and tangled, a strange knotted mess that rests within us.

It's ten years later. That same child is leaning his head against the window. His father is driving the car, and for some reason on that night he decides to ask that question that has been resting within him for so long.

I want to tell him to stop. I already know the answer won't solve anything. But I can't stop it, because it's already happening. It's already happened.

what will they call me when I'm gone

Life isn't chronological.

Am I disappointing? the words slip past his lips and limply fall to the floor of the car, between his worn down sneakers.

About an hour ago, he turned the wheel too fast, or didn't press down fast enough on the brakes. He's not sure. The details are fuzzy. He feels numb, like this is somehow all a dream that he's going to wake up from.

He's felt this way for a while.

When his father answers him, I wish I could overwrite his premeditated laundry list of flaws he's so carefully prepared for his son. I wish I could replace them with the words of comfort that he so desperately needs. I wish I could hold him tight and tell him that this will all make sense later on.

I wish I could tell him that in the end everything turns out okay. But I can't, because even I'm not sure how everything turns out just yet. It hasn't happened yet.

Another ten years have passed. That same child is looking through the car windshield. They want to rest their head. They're tired. They've been tired for a while now.

There's a voice on the radio talking. And somehow even though these are words that were already written, already spoken and recorded, they are words of something that hasn't happened yet. But it's already happened, it always has been.

Life isn't chronological.

It's years later, or maybe years before. The details are fuzzy. Before the car crash, before the bus ride, that same little girl is standing there. Her sisters have put a dress on her, and have begun to excitedly spread make-up across her face.

Their mother tells them to stop. They shouldn't do that, because of course, she's a boy.

To that little girl, I want to ask her, how does this all end? But I'm not sure she knows quite yet, and so instead I decide to leave her with this.

When you get to wherever it is that you're going, call me and I'll meet you there.

Children's Things

Looking at me,
like a dog
that has pissed
on the floor,
I hear
my mother's
scorn.

Do you see this?
she cries
to my father.

I remember him
talking to me
through a crack
in my bedroom door.

It's just not proper.
he explains to me.

So much time
dedicated
to teaching me
what is proper
for a young

boy.

Do not
    hold your hand
that way.

Do not
    sit
that way.

Do not
    stand
that way.

Do not
    dress
that way.

Do not
    think
that your body
is yours to control
    yours to conduct.

And Do not
    question
this foundation
or these thin plaster walls
    might crumble
beneath your glare.

No one can see
    the gay
    or the bi
    in us.

what will they call me when I'm gone

We don't have
the word

Fag

sprawled across
our face.

To be seen
with your,
son
A Man
            inside
                        A Woman's
        dress

How do you hide
                    that

from the shame
and judgment
of others

wondering
what have they done
as parents
to wind up
with a child like
                    that.

someone
who never learned
to put aside those
childish things

of playing
dress-up
as your sisters
spread make-up
across
your face

playing
the mom
in a game
of house.

I follow suit,
collecting these things
and pushing them back
to the recesses
of my mind.

As they threaten to
tumble out
I press
my body
against it
as I pry
the door
shut.

what will they call me when I'm gone

So if when
you look at
her
        as
she
        passes by,
you happen to feel
a yearning,
a muffled memory
of something now lost

do not mind
that tumbling sound
from behind
these thin plaster walls

It's nothing.

        simply
                children's things.

When you hear the chimes ring

Laid open in front of me, I look at the book as I press the little triangle button on my cassette player.

This is the story of Snow White and the Seven Dwarves. You can read along in your book.

You will know it is time to turn the page when you hear the chimes ring like this.

Let's begin now.

Memory works in a funny way. It so often seems like the moments we remember best aren't the ones where we're the happiest. It's the ones that scare us that sear themselves into our mind.

I don't remember the parts of the book where Snow White plays with the forest animals, or laughs and dances with the dwarves. I don't remember the part where the Prince awakens her and they ride away to his castle in the sky.

But I do remember more than anything else, the look of the old witch as she peers into the cottage window. With a deranged look in her eyes and a wide smile, she grips the apple in her hand.

If I close my eyes I can still picture it, as if the book was still there, laid open in front of me.

what will they call me when I'm gone

You will know it is time to turn the page when you hear the chimes ring like this.

Let's begin now.

I'm standing there, looking at my dad through a crack in the door. I'm still wearing the dress.

Are you trying to come out as trans?

His voice sounds tired, almost exasperated. I must have something wrong.

I press rewind and listen back to it.

Are you trying

    trying

Why does he use those words? Why does he use that tone? Maybe there's comfort in there if I listen close enough. There must have been something I missed.

    to come out as trans?

Said as if he's already imagined the yes, and he's pre-exhausted himself by the implications of it. Or maybe he knows the answer is no, but needs to ask as a formality. To get everything aside.

I press rewind again.

Are you

Memory works in a funny way.

The problem with cassette tapes is if you play them over and over again enough times, eventually they begin to wear down. The sounds and voices become distorted, as if the actors need a break from this perpetual cycle.

You will know it is time to turn the page when you hear the chimes ring like this.

I'm still standing there in the door, wearing that dress. I remember the look of my dad as he peers at me through the crack in my door.

I begin to part my lips. I brace myself for my own answer.

You will know it is time to turn the page when you hear the chimes ring like this.

what will they call me when I'm gone

Reflected on the TV screen

My mother
is sitting there
in the family room.

Across from her
on the tv screen
is the image
of Dustin Hoffman.

He's talking about Tootsie.

He's a good deal older now.

The lines on his face
dig a little deeper
than they used to.

He's aged with grace,
as some might say,
in the way that only men
are afforded.

His hair has slightly grayed
but remains as intact
as it always has.

I run my fingers over
the parts of my scalp
that have now smoothed over
with time.

It feels unfair
how our bodies
are always better suited
for situations
before our minds
are prepared for them.

Sitting there
with a confidence and comfort
that has been granted to him,
he says,

Unless I could walk down
the streets of New York
and not have people
turn their heads
and say,

Who's that
guy in drag?

Who's that
freak?

what will they call me when I'm gone

The words linger in the air

I wouldn't do the film.

I wouldn't want the audience
to suspend their
believability.

I think about Tootsie.
about the woman, Tootsie.

about the shape of her face.
the way her glasses rest
on her nose.

how her short curly hair
forms a halo around her head,
keeping form in its resilience.

She looks like a lot of women
I have known.

She looks like my mother.

The image of the two women
are intermingled in my memory.

My mother
is sitting there
watching the image
of this man
across from her.

I sometimes wonder
if he remembers this interview.
if he remembers the tears he shed
in the final moments of it.

I wonder how easy it was for him
to walk away from the role,
to put this aside as just another lesson.

I wonder if it lives with him
as much as it lives with me.

Displayed on the screen,
holding back his tears,
I hear him speak those words.

Now you have me looking like a woman.
Now make me a beautiful woman.
Because I thought I should be beautiful.
If I was going to be a woman
I should be as beautiful
as possible.
And they said to me,
That's as good as it gets.

what will they call me when I'm gone

III
Shifting

Trapped in our own burning

In the blistering heat of our old apartment/ I feel an ache in my chest// there is something wrong with my body// it does not secrete the sweat I so desperately need right now/ instead only delivering that piercing pain to my chest/ like a hard drive that has been so overworked/ that it feels searing to the touch// I stand there in the shower fully clothed/ allowing each fiber to soak in the moisture I so desperately need// soon the heat from within these walls/ will leech from them every droplet they hold/ until I repeat the process again// I think about this building/ creaking/ and slowly/ deteriorating/ in the way that everything and everyone eventually does// I think about what this heat will be/ five years/ ten years/ from now// they say this summer has been the greatest heat wave they have seen// the greatest since last summer// I think about patterns// I think about how the men who built this building/ never intended it for a world like this one/ where we have so slowly trapped ourselves in our own burning// I feel the pain in my chest and notice these fibers do not cling to my skin the way they once did/ the way I so desperately need them to// I feel the cold release from the shower/ the molding wooden window tucked into the corner// something is wrong with my body// it does not produce the sweat I so desperately need.

what will they call me when I'm gone

Phantom limb

He runs his hand down my exposed body and rests it
between my legs,
      asking me to never shave my bush.
I tell him I can not promise him that.

      I think about the last time I laid down
with a man between my legs,
he did it with surgical tools
      to cut deeply, precisely.

I think about that moment and wonder if I should have told
him to cut deeper
      to be a little more reckless with his blade
to cut until nothing remained there
      nothing but a sense
    of who everyone once
thought me to be.

As I lay there on that bed
      I imagine shaving it down,
smoothing it down for the doctors
      to make their cuts
    and corrections.

When that man in the bed wraps his hand around
      that phantom limb,
when his lips encompass it
      I wish I could say I feel that ecstasy of pleasure
he so strongly wishes to wring out of me

and yet the sensation feels numb
    like a memory
        long since faded away.

In this moment I hope to be a faded memory
    of my future self,
      my past form
conjuring up only fog in the minds of others

to be scrubbed away,
shaved down,
and cut clean.

what will they call me when I'm gone

Someone That Was

Over time
the cells
that make up
our bodies
die
and regenerate

every fragment
replacing the last
until nothing
of the past
remains

We are
composed completely
of memories
of our former selves,
wrinkled and creased
from being
stretched and folded
again
and again

I look
at a picture
of myself
as a young boy,
hair like
straws of hay
draped limply
over my head.

This photo,
is light captured
in a fleeting moment,
then pressed and stained
into wood
that has been

processed and bleached

to create
a representation,
an illusion,
of someone
that was.

what will they call me when I'm gone

Moments like these

I'm sitting there on the toilet looking at my reflection in the mirror as tears run down my face. Christina Aguilera is playing from the speakers of my phone. I can't decide if this is poetic or just pathetic. Maybe it's a bit of both.

The song is *Reflection*, which might be the most embarrassing part. Breakdowns shouldn't be so corporate. My life shouldn't be so hackneyed and trite.

I picture this as a scene from some Oscar bait drama from ten years ago. The cool indie dvd store, the one next to that coffee shop, shelve it in the queer section next to *Boys Don't Cry* and *The Danish Girl*.

Some liberal middle aged mom calls the movie eye opening as she talks to her friends over a glass of red wine at their weekly book club. She puts a pride flag outside her house to show that she's an ally, though to be honest, she admits to her friends, she's not really sure she even knows that many gay people. The conversation turns to Trump. They talk about opening another bottle of wine.

One of the things about being closeted, even so deeply closeted that you don't even know it yourself, is that other people figure it out anyway.

My coworker is telling me that I'm a faggot and that I'm going to burn in hell.

We're in the back of a *Pizza Hut*. I'm doing prep work because it's the only thing I'm competent at. I'm working two jobs and in my exhausted state I'm glad that this is the one I see far less.

He tells me that when I die, they're going to bury me in a dress. He laughs at his own joke.

Sitting here on the toilet, I pray that he's right.

what will they call me when I'm gone

Flowing/shifting

The reflection in the mirror/ pale and malformed/ like flowing water that has yet to take shape/ in a body of its own// at least when you look/ in a funhouse mirror/ there is a shared acknowledgment/ that what you're seeing/ is some form of distortion// have you ever looked at water/ once it is frozen/ no/ not ice/ don't call it ice/ this state is only temporary/ it still has so far to go// sometimes/ when you really stop/ to look/ you can see the bubbles// have a sense of how it once flowed/ where it has melted and reshaped itself// I run my eyes across my body/ the stretches and marks/ signs of its former forms// I don't want to call it a body// this is just a temporary state// the water that composes us/ that runs through our body/ is that same water that ran through/ those bodies before our own// freezing/ shaping/ melting/ flowing/ rising up/ and composing those clouds/ those same clouds you saw as a child/ as you held your mother's hand// as that distorted reflection looks back at me/ I remember/ that we are still freezing/ flowing/ shaping/ rising up to form those clouds// so when you look up/ at those clouds/ those wondrous figures/ that hang in the sky/ those are our reflections/ always flowing/ always shifting.

what will they call me when I'm gone

IV
Changing

Reverent silence

As that first streak
of light and color
rises up
into the sky,
a silence
ripples out
among the crowd.

They know
that bang,
that sudden flash of light,
only has meaning
when it is enveloped
by reverent silence.

I think about reverence,
about Paul Revere,
about the red, white, and blue,
bodies,
bruised and blue.

I think about fireworks.
About how they're never worth
everything they cost.

Animals in their panic
flee from their family.
A small child
is left lost and alone.

what will they call me when I'm gone

Tomorrow I will read
about the White House,
about Biden,
about people protesting
for the rights and voices
of children.

But right now
I stand here
among the crowd
shrouded in silence
as I whisper
a secret truth
to and from myself.

A truth nestled
so deeply in darkness
that only now
do I allow myself
to silently share it.

As the group walks home
I talk to a woman
about her bag,
about this city,
about the nearby theater.

I make the joke
that I've never seen
Rocky Horror
out of fear
of what I may discover
about myself.

She laughs,
but I know
that joke
is outdated.

After we part
I walk the rest
of the way home
enveloped
in reverent silence,

waiting for that bang,
that sudden flash of light.

what will they call me when I'm gone

The deafening sound

He shot her corpse

long after he knew
she was dead.

Long after
he had left her there
lying lifeless on the ground.

He wanted to make clear,
not her death,
but how much he hated
her life,
her existence

with each bullet
punctuating
his disgust

mangling her corpse,
her body,
long after
it could have been said
to be a person.

You hear things like that
and you want to believe
that the world mourns with you.

You want to believe that the world
shares your tears.

I want to hush it out.
the cries,
the condemnations,
the celebration
of the fact
that this woman breathed
the last few breaths of her life.

With each word
I hear that gunfire
ring through the air,
punctuating
her death,
their hatred
for her life
again,
and again

making sure
that it echoes.

    it echoes
so loudly.

No,
no,
not an echo.

what will they call me when I'm gone

Echoes fade.

This only gets louder,
and louder,
as a woman,
the person that she was,
fades from existence.

They keep telling me
that those gunshots
aren't there.

That there's nothing out there.
That these are figments of my mind.

They tell me as if their voices
of reassurance
can drown out
the deafening sound
of her corpse
being riddled again and again.

I know what I hear.
I know what I feel.

Sometimes,
I wonder
when my body lies there
when my body can no longer
be said to be me,
what words will echo,
what words will be used
to punctuate
or to erase
my existence.

I can still hear the gunshots.

They're getting louder.

what will they call me when I'm gone

Little Inconveniences

      I'm sitting there
when they bring him up

The man who plunged his car
into the cold water,

the one who drove it
off the bridge.

She's talking about it
with this irritation
in her voice.

        People do things
        like that,

she says

        When they have
        all these services

        to support them

I'm sitting there
with the phone in my hand

as the person
on the other line
tries to talk me down.

The phrase
      mechanical teddy bear
crosses my mind

I wonder
how he felt
when he hit the water.

Did it pierce his skin
jolting him awake
like a cold shower
in the morning?

Did it wrap around him
like a welcoming blanket?

Do you ever wonder
what little inconveniences
your death might cause?

People muttering
as you're late for work.

Your landlord
still asking for the rent.

Someone has to carry you
out of there

a rotting collection
of unpaid debts
and broken promises.

what will they call me when I'm gone

I hope when he hit the water
it meant something.

I hope it meant
  the world to him.

whatever that world
might look like.

what will they call me when I'm gone

V
Rising

The con

She starts the sentence and before it is done,
    I know exactly how it will end
        because I have heard this same phrase
                with the same cadence
so many times before.
Prepackaged for your convenience to be parroted off
whenever necessary,
Pre-fabricated,
Pre-constructed
so you do not have to think about the meaning
that these words might hold
as they emit from your mouth
when you mindlessly mimic this memetic memo
as if your mouth was a *Memorex.*

        "Won't all of this talk
    about gender
        leave these kids
           confused?"
That word,
    confused
that so perfectly and purposefully punctuates that phrase
    has a whole other life and meaning than the one we
have come to know.

what will they call me when I'm gone

No, confused is not the temporary state of mind
            as we gradually
                gain grains of knowledge
seeds to be
            sown and grown
No, here in this carefully constructed slogan
                        confused does not
            mean to grow
            but to be groomed

Whether this is known or intended by the speaker
as the words
                graze against their lips
is irrelevant.

It is made so that they do not have to know or think,
like carriers of the common cold
it will spread
regardless of if it is done with
        a cough or a kiss.

Unknowing or unwilling
to   admit,
to commit
to the truth
that the confusion is what
                        they
                    carry
                        within
                            them.

In the hopes to sustain and spread
this solipsistic saying
to spread this idea that
to be confused is
to be corrupted,
to be perverted
to stray
too far from the mold that has been carved for you.

I know what it's like
to be confused.
I am an expert,
            No
      a connoisseur of
         confusion

I have been
      Confused as to why my mother
tells me not to hold my hand
a certain way.

      Confused as to why my classmates
tell me not to sit
a certain way.

      Confused as to why my own parents
are afraid to be seen with me dressed
a certain way.

what will they call me when I'm gone

confused as to why I feel so
confined and
constrained by this
construction.

A construction made to
    contain and retain me in this state of
    confusion

Thirty years I have known
confused
so trust me when I say
    I   know
confused
    inside
            and out.

So do not talk about it
as if it is some boogeyman
that comes into the night
to snatch your children away

Nights like the ones
I have spent
asking God
        What is wrong with me?

Nights where my brain
            has been trained
to not ask the essential questions
            that contain
        the essence
        of escape
from these clumsily
                construed
                confines.

Despite the weights
        and constraints
I have been unknowingly shackled with
    you could not contain me in
            my confusion.

And consequently,
I will
 not continue
    to contain
others in your own
        confusion

So trust me that when I say all this
from the chasms of my chest
from the belly of my beating heart.

We
        are
            not
                confused.

                    what will they call me when I'm gone

See How We Bleed

The conversation has turned
to the topic of bleeding
and cramping,
to monthly rituals.

She places
a patronizing hand
on my shoulder
and with a curled up smile
says to me,

Be glad you're not a woman.

Splayed out in front of you
in your high school textbook
is what we have called
the female anatomy.

Lines jut out from it
like flags planted in the ground.
Plots of land,
colonized,
marked and named
by the men who claimed
to have
discovered them.

Lauren Scott   70

Like the Europeans
who came to these shores
so many years ago,
          there's a special kind of arrogance
to men
who believe
that something does not exist
until they have given a name to it.

In class
they teach you the names.
they teach you the parts.
they tell you
                    This is a woman.

they tell you about the bleeding.
about the cramps.

It's easy to talk about that bleeding.
It's easy to talk about
the pain and hardships
of femininity
when they have laid it out
so clearly
in the textbooks.

The pain
that your coworker,
      your friend,
      your brother,
will acknowledge
with little resistance.

what will they call me when I'm gone

He'll see how you bleed
in the way the textbooks
told him to.

You tell him
because he won't see,
        refuses to see
the thousands of other ways
in which we bleed.

The thousand tiny, little
microscopic cuts
slowly set into you
each day.

The cuts they make
with their voice
when it
intrudes on your own.

The cuts they make
with their eyes
when they
look at you
a little too long,
look with
a little too much hunger.

Cuts made
by the way their hands pry,
by the way their tongues lie.

Cuts made
in ways they'll never tell
        they'll never teach.

Lauren Scott   72

And so you speak
in the ways they teach.

A pinhole made
in the bag
they have placed around
your face.

And so when I speak
and say that I am a woman,
I cannot blame you
for feeling like I have placed
my cold hand
over your last vestiges
of air.

To feel that when I speak
that I am yet another colonizer
grinding the heels of their boots
into the earth of your soil.

the way in which we bleed,
the way in which the bodies
of my sisters bleed
as they lie in the streets
will not be written in the textbooks,
will not be taught within those walls.

what will they call me when I'm gone

Forgive me.
I do not mean
to paint a picture of femininity
solely with blood,
pain,
and anguish.

I do not mean
to wash over
and erase the joys
of womanhood.

There are moments of joy,
but maybe those are best left
for another time.

In the meantime,
let us write
in our blood.

Let us show them
how we bleed.

Ordinary boy

When I think about gender,
When I think about transness,
      I think about the Disney film, *Pinocchio*.

Now let me stop you there, because I can sense your mind
trying to rush ahead of mine in an attempt to piece together
this narrative before the words have even left my mouth.

And maybe in the eyes of your cisgendered mind you have
weaved a tale where this little wooden Italian boy is our sad
and lowly trans folk, while the humans of flesh and blood
who breathe and eat?
      Why of course they must be you.
How could they not?

And how could poor Pinocchio not wish to be one of you,
eagerly waiting for a blue fairy to come and finally make him
real?

And if this is presumptuous, forgive me, but through my time
and experience I have become intimately familiar with the
simple tale told to appease so many cis people. Of a young
boy staring into a mirror, wishing to be a girl, knowing since
birth that they were born into the wrong body.

Reductive, patronizing yarns that try not to challenge your
little minds too much.

But I can assure you, none of these hackneyed cliches
describe my life, and I wait for no blue fairy to make me real,
for you can look at me now and see I am as real as I have
ever been.

No, when I think of Pinocchio, I think of his song,

    I've Got No Strings

Where he joyfully stumbles and trips, yet in those flaws,
there is an idiosyncratic beauty. Those other puppets, bound
to an unseen hand, do not have the agency,
                     the awareness

to waste energy on questions of why, and can in that, afford
to be flawless but thoughtless in their performance.

But, our hero exists in that in between and there is
something so mesmerizing and transcendent about existing
within that elusive space.

Maybe now it is clicking into your mind what your role in
this story is:
        a puppet bound by strings.

And if you feel objectified by this, if you feel otherized, do not
worry, this feeling will pass, and if it doesn't,

you will grow accustomed to it.

But let's go back to that initial narrative, the one your mind might have so readily clicked to, where this boy of wood and paint, so eagerly wished to be where you are now. I'm willing to bet in your mind you already have a clear idea of the puppet: the color of his hat and the cut of his vest. But I want you to take a moment and close your eyes. Try to remember what he looks like after the blue fairy has granted his wish and he is made from skin and bone.

Maybe you can remember,
            but didn't it take you a moment?
When you could so easily remember that sad wooden boy.

I think we both know the reason why.

No one wants to see a tale of an ordinary boy,
and I can assure you,

I am no ordinary boy.

The question they never ask

I still spend most of my days,
presenting myself,
        as a man.

But lately,
I've been starting to tell people
that I am
        a trans woman.

Usually this prompts the same questions
        the same responses.

        When are you starting hormones?
        Are you going to get all of the operations?

I'm curious what they mean by
        all of the operations.
A part of me is tempted to ask them.
        to list of those said
                operations.

But they never ask me the question
I really want to answer.
        What's it like to be trans?

And I know why they don't ask me.
It's because they think they already have the answer.

Lauren Scott   78

It's that simple phrase
we've heard time
      and time again.

I was born in the wrong body

I'm not sure who started that phrase,
but I'll let you know,
      I'm ending it here.

So because you won't ask me
I'll ask it for you,
and I'll even
answer it for you too.

So,
    what's it like to be trans?

I want you to imagine,

and I phrase this for the cis women,
but for my cis men,
if you want to,
you can flip it
to better suit yourself.

I want you to imagine,
living a year as a man,
as if you've been one for your entire life.

what will they call me when I'm gone

And no one remembers the past version of you.
No one but you.

This is the name and face
that everyone has always known you by.
Your friends, your family, your coworkers,
the person who makes your coffee in the morning.

And when I ask you to imagine that year,
don't just gloss over it
in that way I know you are so tempted to do.
don't just think about the first morning.

Think about the days,
        about the weeks,
                about the months.

I want you to think about the hours,
                about the minutes,
as they crawl by second by second.

You remind yourself that by the end of the year
it will all be over, and you can go back
        to the way things were.

Then as those last few days of December come around,
they tell you
that you have to do it
        for another three years.

So you do it again.

You've done it before.

It's just a little longer this time.

Then it's another five.

After a certain point,
you forget what you were
        counting down to.

You know you had a different name before. You just can't
remember what it was.
It's on the tip of your tongue.
If only you heard it, then you could remember it,
but it's been so, so long since you heard it.

        What was that name again?

And you start to feel a little numb. Like you just woke up
from a nap, or maybe like you haven't woken up yet, and this
is still all a dream, but you know it's not, because it can't be,
because that doesn't make any sense.

        Nothing makes any sense.

And you feel like you're empty somehow, almost hollow, like
you're missing something, but you're not quite sure what
that something is.

        what will they call me when I'm gone

And then one day,
you hear something.
Something so familiar.
It's like the tune to a song you just can't name
or a dream that you swear you've had
so many times before.

It's a voice.

It's a voice you haven't heard in a long time.

It's the voice that comes out
when you're caught off guard

or when you want to let your waitress know
that you really do want her to have a good day.

It's the voice of a little girl
crying

because she's so scared and alone,
because she's been neglected and forgotten
for so long.

And in that moment,
when you find her
after all these years,
you hold her tight,
as tight as possible,
because you want her to know
that you will never let go again.

You will never forget about her again.
Never neglect her.
Never let her have to reside
in the dark recesses of that closet.

And you hate yourself.
        You hate yourself so much.
For every time you didn't hear her murmured cries
muffled from behind those thin plaster walls.

For every moment you lost with her.
For every day you didn't spend together.
For every day she had to spend alone and scared.

And as you wipe away her tears,
and listen as her cries die down
you realize
            that was you crying
all along.

You just muffled it,
behind these walls.

And suddenly there's this silence,
this clarity,
and everything
comes rushing back to you.

And sure,
it will take some time
to remember the little things.

Remembering how to talk again.

Remembering how to walk again.

But you'll be with that little girl,
learning with her
every step of the way.

So don't ask me
about the hormones
or the operations.

Don't ask me about any of this shit
that doesn't really matter.

I wasn't born into the wrong body,

as if there's some other unused
collection of flesh and bone
lying around
like a misplaced set of keys
or a forgotten pair of shoes.

I wasn't born into the wrong body.

I was forced into the wrong life.

Vandalize my grave

I miss the days
        of not caring
when
    and how
        I died.

It's so much easier
    to let go
of your sense
        of self
when you have no
        sense of

    self.

Not caring
    how I would be dressed
or what
    words
they would print in the
        obituary.

So when I say this,
I say it not as a simple
        passing thought,
or as a   sweet nothing
to momentarily rest
in your mouth
before   it melts away.

what will they call me when I'm gone

Instead,
I say this
as a manifesto
to be chiseled
into these pages,
and embedded
into your mind.

If you are to see
in my obituary,
the words
          brother
                    or son
singed into
my desecrated corpse,
know that those
who claim to   mourn me,
have never   known me.

If they are to mark
my false name
into that stone,
know that is
               not
                     my
                         grave

but a phantom figment
of a person
that never was.

Have my name
writ large
in red
across that stone.

Do not
bring flowers
        to that grave.

Do not
spread
        my ashes.

Spread
        My word
        My name.

Let it ring
        in the ears
of all that hear.

Let it burn
        into the iris
of all that read.

Too many of our brothers
have had their legacies buried
as people lay upon their coffin
words like daughter,
words like wife.

Too many of our sisters
have been forsaken

what will they call me when I'm gone

as their lives
are surreptitiously erased
as those who can still stand
            can still speak
desecrate the dead
with words
that envelop
      their bodies,
in ways
      that their silent skins
are forced to
   succumb to.

If I lay there
            as they speak,
do not let those words
pass their lips
without refutation,
without indignation.

Do not let them
bury me
with those words.

If my words,
        my pages
are to be
the final mark
that I lay upon
this world,

Let them not
be words
that surrender to
the shadows.

Let these words
be my life,
be my casket,
be my tomb.

Let them be
my legacy.

what will they call me when I'm gone

what
will they
call me
when
I'm gone

Colophon

The Wider Perspectives Colophon page has been reworked and reworked to try to accommodate the ever growing list of authors represented. It is a reflection of the pen-to-paper and often aloud-presented talent in the Hampton Roads area of Southeast Virginia. This page used to have many cute and poetic expressions, but the sheer number of quality artists deserving mention has become some serious business. Voices shouldn't be silenced any more than experiences should be discounted. The book that will save your life is waiting for you from one of these authors!!

Luana LU Portales   Ken Sutton

Samantha Casey   Sonya Fitch

Chris (thePoeticGenius) Green

Donna Burnett-Robinson

Faith May Griffin

Se'Mon-Michelle Rosser

Lisa M. Kendrick

Brittiny Gardner   Charles Wilson

Cassandra IsFree

Nich (Nicholis Williams)

Samantha Geovjian Clarke

Natalie Morison-Uzzle

Gus Woodward II

Brandi Dise   Jack Cassada

Patsy Bickerstaff

Dezz   Grey Hues

(Doowrag) Daniel Garwood

Jada Hollingsworth

Tabetha Moon House

Nick Marickovich

Madeline Garcia (Maddie G.)

Chichi Iwuorie   Rivers Raye

Symay Rhodes   Terra Leigh

Tanya Cunningham (Scientific Eve)

Raymond M. Simmons

S.A. Borders-Shoemaker

Taz Weysweete'

Ann Shalaski   Serena Fusek

Jade Leonard   Darean Polk

Bobby K. (The Poor Man's Poet)

J. Scott Wilson (Teech!)

Gloria Darlene Mann

Neil Spirtas   Edith Blake

Don (Bent Spoke) MacKellar

Jorge Mendez & JT Williams

Sarah Eileen Mendez (Williams)

Stephanie Diana (Noftz)

Shanya – Lady S.

Jason Brown (Drk Mtr)

Kailyn Rae Sasso

Crickyt J. Expression

Toni Lynn Britton

Morgan Guyton (Starchild)

Faith Clay (Arlandria Speaks)

Talis Matreshka   Luna Monet Sierra

Chris Will Hardy

Erato -the Muse (Oliver Chauncey-Heine)

Jason Williams Willy-Jay

Easter PoetikDesire Dodds

Crystal Nolen   Zach Crowe

James Harry Wilson

Catherine TL Hodges

Martina Champion

Kent Knowlton   Vanessa Jones

Tony Broadway   Maria April C.

Mark Willoughby

Linda Spence-Howard

the Hampton Roads Artistic Collective (757 Perspectives) & The Poet's Domain are all WPP literary journals in cooperation with Scientific Eve or Live Wire Press

Check for those artists on FaceBook, Instagram, the Virginia Poetry Online channel on YouTube, and other social media. Please check out how *They art...*

www.ingramcontent.com/pod-product-compliance
Lightning Source LLC
Chambersburg PA
CBHW071158090426
42736CB00012B/2378